NATIONAL
GEOGRAPHIC

At the Farmer's Market

Myles James

I am going to the farmer's market.
I have some money to spend.

I want to buy a carrot
for my rabbit.
I will need these coins.

How much does the carrot cost?

I want to buy a flower
for my grandmother.
I will need these coins.

How much does the flower cost?

I want to buy an apple
for my brother.
I will need these coins.

How much does the apple cost?

sale

I want to buy a plant
for my father.
I will need these coins.

How much does the plant cost?

I want to buy some honey
for my mother.
I will need these coins.

How much does the honey cost?

I want to buy a cake
for myself.
I will need these coins.

How much does the cake cost?

Carrot	10¢
Flower	35¢
Apple	50¢
Plant	70¢
Honey	85¢
Cake	95¢